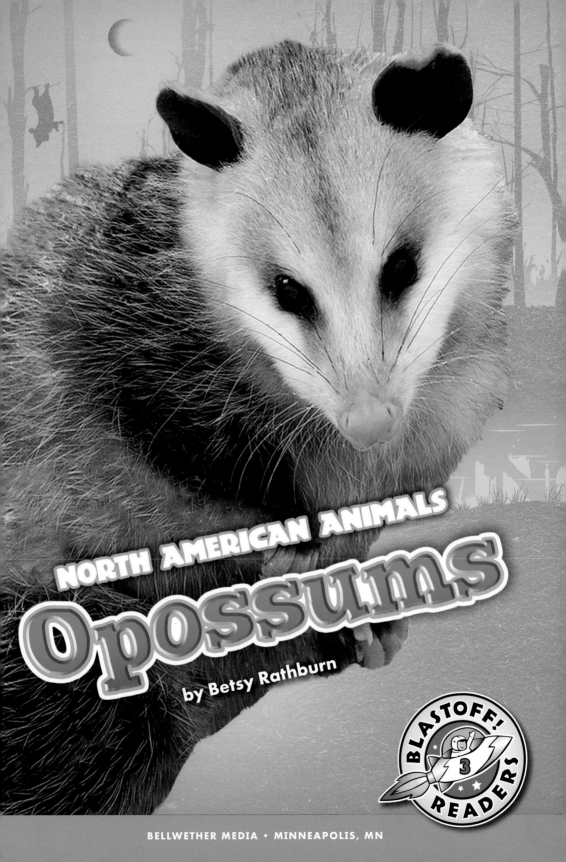

NORTH AMERICAN ANIMALS
Opossums

by Betsy Rathburn

BELLWETHER MEDIA • MINNEAPOLIS, MN

Note to Librarians, Teachers, and Parents:

Blastoff! Readers are carefully developed by literacy experts and combine standards-based content with developmentally appropriate text.

Level 1 provides the most support through repetition of high-frequency words, light text, predictable sentence patterns, and strong visual support.

Level 2 offers early readers a bit more challenge through varied simple sentences, increased text load, and less repetition of high-frequency words.

Level 3 advances early-fluent readers toward fluency through increased text and concept load, less reliance on visuals, longer sentences, and more literary language.

Level 4 builds reading stamina by providing more text per page, increased use of punctuation, greater variation in sentence patterns, and increasingly challenging vocabulary.

Level 5 encourages children to move from "learning to read" to "reading to learn" by providing even more text, varied writing styles, and less familiar topics.

Whichever book is right for your reader, Blastoff! Readers are the perfect books to build confidence and encourage a love of reading that will last a lifetime!

This edition first published in 2018 by Bellwether Media, Inc.

No part of this publication may be reproduced in whole or in part without written permission of the publisher. For information regarding permission, write to Bellwether Media, Inc., Attention: Permissions Department, 5357 Penn Avenue South, Minneapolis, MN 55419.

Library of Congress Cataloging-in-Publication Data

Names: Rathburn, Betsy, author.
Title: Opossums / by Betsy Rathburn.
Description: Minneapolis, MN : Bellwether Media, Inc., 2018. | Series: Blastoff! Readers. North American Animals | Audience: Age 5-8. | Audience: K to Grade 3. | Includes bibliographical references and index.
Identifiers: LCCN 2017028789 | ISBN 9781626177291 (hardcover : alk. paper) | ISBN 9781681034706 (ebook)
Subjects: LCSH: Opossums–Juvenile literature. | CYAC: Opossums.
Classification: LCC QL737.M34 R38 2018 | DDC 599.2/76–dc23
LC record available at https://lccn.loc.gov/2017028789

Editor: Rebecca Sabelko   Designer: Josh Brink
Printed in the United States of America, North Mankato, MN.

Table of Contents

What Are Opossums?

Opossums are the only **marsupials** in North America. These **mammals** are known for their fur-lined pouches.

In the Wild

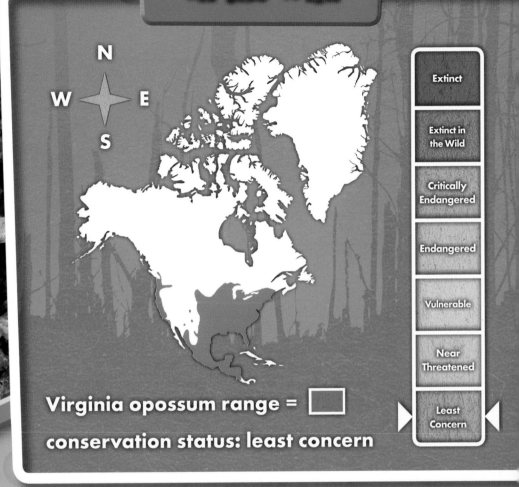

N
W   E
S

Extinct

Extinct in the Wild

Critically Endangered

Endangered

Vulnerable

Near Threatened

Least Concern

Virginia opossum range = ☐

conservation status: least concern

Opossums live from Canada to **Central America**. There are many types. Virgina opossums are among the most common.

5

Opossums have many different **habitats**. In forests, they stay hidden in tree roots, hollow stumps, and treetops.

Opossums live in cities, too. They look for food in parks and backyards.

Opposable Opossums

Opossums are good climbers. **Opposable toes** and sharp claws help them **grip** branches.

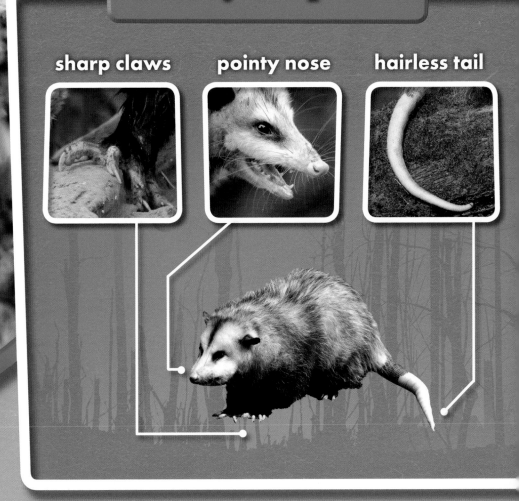

Identify an Opossum

sharp claws **pointy nose** **hairless tail**

Opossums grip with their tails, too. They can even use them to carry twigs and leaves!

Opossums are covered in grayish black fur. But their ears and tails are hairless.

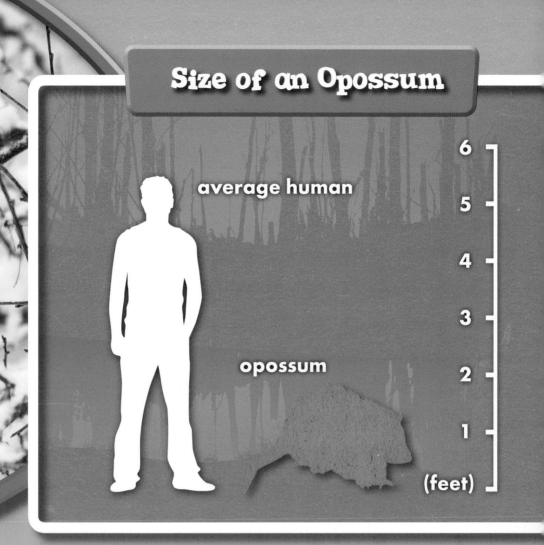

Size of an Opossum

average human

opossum

6
5
4
3
2
1
(feet)

Dark eyes peer out above opossums' pointy noses. The animals can grow up to 3.2 feet (1 meter) long from nose to tail.

Opossums have many **predators**. Eagles and owls often carry them away. On the ground, foxes, coyotes, and bobcats are common enemies.

gray foxes

great horned owls

bobcats

coyotes

bald eagles

snapping turtles

Sometimes, opossums have to fight off rattlesnakes! But they are not hurt by rattlesnake **venom**.

When they are in danger,
opossums may pretend to be
dead. They drop to the ground
and stay still until they are safe.

Other times, they hiss and screech. They show their teeth to scare away enemies.

Opossums are not picky eaters. These **omnivores** eat fruit, insects, and small animals. Sometimes, they even steal pet food.

acorns

pigeons

deer ticks

field crickets

blackberries

crayfish

Opossums search for food at night. These **nocturnal** critters are often found digging through trash cans!

Tiny Babies

Once or twice a year, female opossums have around eight **joeys**. These tiny babies are born with no fur. They crawl into their mom's warm pouch. There, the joeys **nurse** for about three months.

Baby Facts

Name for babies:	joeys
Size of litter:	7 to 8 joeys
Length of pregnancy:	12 to 13 days
Time spent with mom:	about 3 months

When the joeys are bigger,
they crawl out of the pouch.
They ride on mom's back as
she searches for food.

After another month, the joeys are ready to explore!

Glossary

Central America—the narrow, southern part of North America

grip—to hold tightly

habitats—lands with certain types of plants, animals, and weather

joeys—baby opossums

mammals—warm-blooded animals that have backbones and feed their young milk

marsupials—mammals that carry their young in a pouch

nocturnal—active at night

nurse—to drink mom's milk

omnivores—animals that eat both plants and animals

opposable toes—toes that can be moved to touch the other toes on the same foot; opossums have opposable toes on their back feet.

predators—animals that hunt other animals for food

venom—poison created by rattlesnakes

To Learn More

AT THE LIBRARY

Berne, Emma Carlson. *Opossums.* New York, N.Y.: PowerKids Press, 2015.

Quinlivan, Ada. *Opossums.* New York, N.Y.: PowerKids Press, 2017.

Tatlock, Ann. *Opossums.* Kennett Square, Pa.: Purple Toad Publishing, Inc., 2015.

ON THE WEB

Learning more about opossums is as easy as 1, 2, 3.

1. Go to www.factsurfer.com.

2. Enter "opossums" into the search box.

3. Click the "Surf" button and you will see a list of related web sites.

With factsurfer.com, finding more information is just a click away.

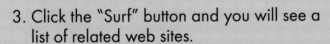

Index

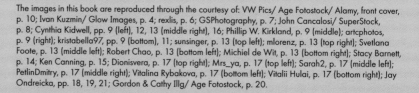

The images in this book are reproduced through the courtesy of: VW Pics/ Age Fotostock/ Alamy, front cover, p. 10; Ivan Kuzmin/ Glow Images, p. 4; rexlis, p. 6; GSPhotography, p. 7; John Cancalosi/ SuperStock, p. 8; Cynthia Kidwell, pp. 9 (left), 12, 13 (middle right), 16; Phillip W. Kirkland, p. 9 (middle); artcphotos, p. 9 (right); kristabella97, pp. 9 (bottom), 11; sunsinger, p. 13 (top left); mlorenz, p. 13 (top right); Svetlana Foote, p. 13 (middle left); Robert Chao, p. 13 (bottom left); Michiel de Wit, p. 13 (bottom right); Stacy Barnett, p. 14; Ken Canning, p. 15; Dionisvera, p. 17 (top right); Mrs_ya, p. 17 (top left); Sarah2, p. 17 (middle left); PetlinDmitry, p. 17 (middle right); Vitalina Rybakova, p. 17 (bottom left); Vitalii Hulai, p. 17 (bottom right); Jay Ondreicka, pp. 18, 19, 21; Gordon & Cathy Illg/ Age Fotostock, p. 20.